1981

TEAM UP

FOR BETTER TEACHING

by Betty N. Chase

illustrated by Max Kennedy

STANDARD PUBLISHING
Cincinnati, Ohio   **3242**

ISBN: 0-87239-114-0

Library of Congress Catalog Card Number: 76-19876

CONTENTS

WHAT IS TEAM TEACHING?

m teaching is....

the combined efforts of two or more teachers sharing the responsibility for teaching a group of learners.

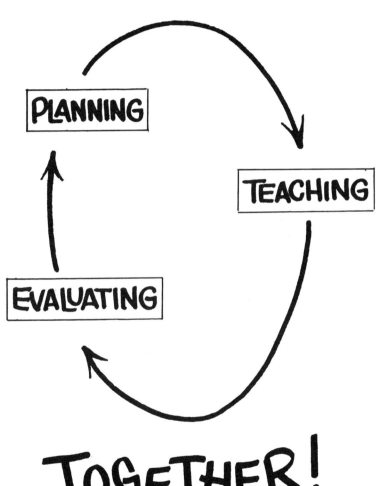

Team Teaching involves:

PLANNING

TEACHING

EVALUATING

TOGETHER!

There is a difference between team teaching and just taking turns teaching.

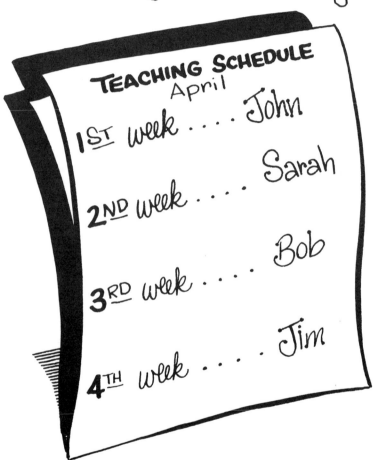

TEACHING SCHEDULE
April

1ST week . . . . . John

2ND week . . . . . Sarah

3RD week . . . . Bob

4TH week . . . . . Jim

Just because two teachers are in a room together, does not mean they are a teaching team.

A Teaching team has been created when two or more teachers not only share a room, but also **Plan their lessons TOGETHER.**

A smaller, more informal team may have only two people working together.

A husband and wife teaching together create a very effective team. They can study and plan in their home as their schedule is free during the week.

Leadership and secretarial responsibilities can be shared on a team of two because less formal organization is required.

However, if a team grows to three or more teachers, the department needs a person to be the Department Leader. Also a separate person is needed to be Department Secretary.

Therefore, responsibilities are divided and there is more efficiency.

As a team grows, three
roles become necessary
on a teaching team...

...a Department Leader

...Teachers

...Department
Secretary

First there are...

Teachers

The teachers are responsible for planning, teaching, and evaluating together.

Each teacher is assigned
a small class of 8-10 learners.

Teachers **PLAN** together.
They Prepare for planning sessions by...

1. Studying the Scripture for the lesson.

2. Jotting down all ideas.

3. Skimming all of the teachers' resources.

Teachers TEACH together. Each teacher carries out his responsibility in that lesson to the best of his ability.

Finally, teachers **EVALUATE** together...

... whether the AIM was reached

...the response of the learners

...their teaching techniques

One of the teachers is selected as a...

...Department Leader

The Department Leader
is a leader of teachers.
He is usually the most
highly skilled teacher on
the team.

The Department Leader plans, teaches, and evaluates with his teachers.

However, the Department Leader also has administrative duties like...

...Scheduling weekly planning meetings,

... Guiding discussion during the planning sessions,

25

...Watching class size and recruiting a new teacher, if necessary,

. . . Making changes in the timing of the lesson, if necessary.

We haven't finished. Could we have five more minutes?

. . . Being aware of special needs and feelings of each team member

Because he has many administrative duties, the Department Leader usually does not have a class assigned to him.

However, he functions as a teacher in some of the department activities.

Finally, each team needs a
Department SECRETARY

The secretary greets students,

. . .Takes attendance for all classes within the department,

...Takes the offering by means of an offering plate near the door,

...Registers visitors to the department and assigns them to a class,

... and helps teachers with follow-up contacts by addressing postcards and papers to absentees.

Therefore, a teaching team Consists of...

Department Leader

Teachers

Department Secretary

... All with the common goal of leading learners to Christ and helping them mature as Christians.

Grouping for a Team Approach

A teaching team uses a combination of class activities and department activities.

... A CLASS CONSISTS OF 8-10 LEARNERS

... A DEPARTMENT CONSISTS OF 20-40 LEARNERS

There may be anywhere from 2-5 classes in one department.

* DEPARTMENT
(24-40 LEARNERS)

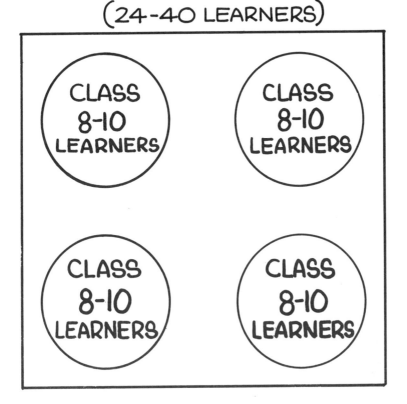

CLASS
8-10
LEARNERS

CLASS
8-10
LEARNERS

CLASS
8-10
LEARNERS

CLASS
8-10
LEARNERS

Personnel for Department
1 Department Leader
4 Teachers
1 Secretary

Department time consists of all classes in one large group.

DEPARTMENT TIME
can be used for...

...illustrated lectures to introduce a unit or lesson,

...for special speakers,

...for showing a film or filmstrip that is appropriate to the lesson aim,

...for singing songs or hymns that are appropriate to your lesson aim,

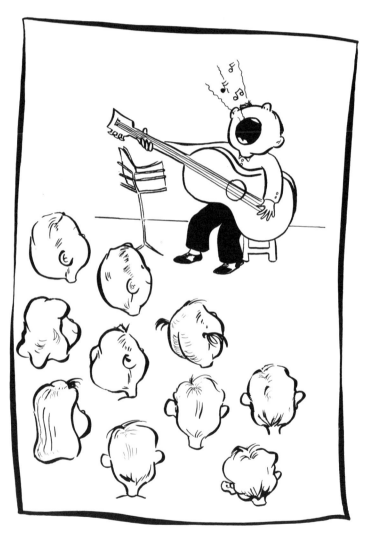

...for reports from small-group discussions,

...as an audience for presentation of class projects.

Class time consists of small groups of 8-10 learners studying with their own teacher.

CLASS TIME
Can be utilized for...

Studying the Bible through discussion,

...studying the Bible through art activities,

...Studying the Bible through creative writing,

...Studying the Bible through preparing music activities,

...Studying the Bible through skits and plays,

...Studying the Bible through research activities.

However, so that learners are relating to one teacher closely, use 70-80% of the total time for class time and only 20-30% of the time in Department time.

A combination of class time and department time adds variety to your lesson plan and also makes the best use of each teacher's time.

Facilities

Although facilities have the **least** important influence on your educational program, facilities do have some effect on the church's teaching ministry.

Traditionally, facilities have looked like this:

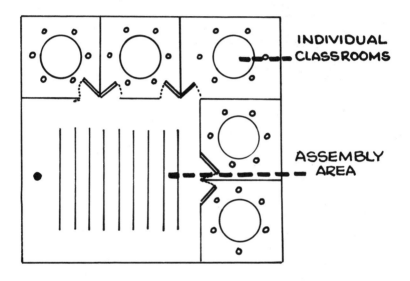

INDIVIDUAL CLASSROOMS

ASSEMBLY AREA

There was an Opening exercise in the assembly area, then class time in the small rooms. This is called a classroom-assembly arrangement.

Newer facilities look like this:

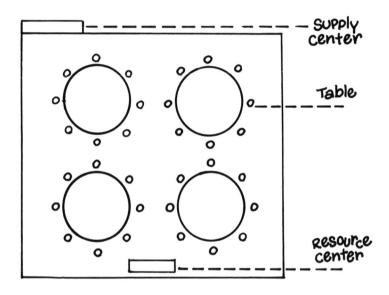

This is called an open room arrangement.

Advantages of an Open room arrangement are:

CHECK LIST

- ☑ Less expensive to build
- ☑ Multipurpose
- ☑ Greater flexibility in teaching methods
- ☑ Greater flexibility in grouping students
- ☑ Less time wasted in shifting classes
- ☑ Fewer discipline problems (this may be hard to believe, but observe a team approach and you'll find this to be true!)
- ☑ Resources available to teachers and students in the department.

Old facilities can be easily adapted for large and small groups by...

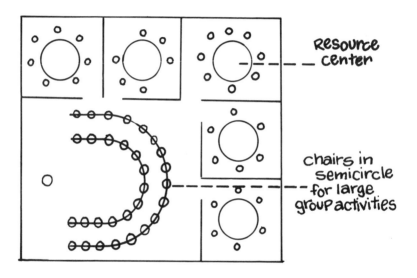

Resource center

chairs in semicircle for large group activities

... Removing doors so that the small rooms appear more open

... Removing walls (if possible)

For the younger age levels, facilities can be adapted like this:

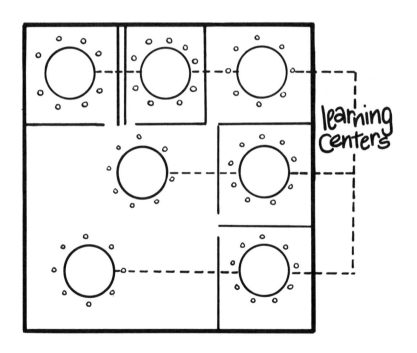

learning centers

If you would like to use a team approach, open room facilities are good to have.

But they are the least important factor. The _enthusiasm_ of a teacher is the major factor in a class room.

Utilizing Total Session Teaching

A child spends approximately 800 hours in public school each year.

That same child spends Only 52 hours a year in Sunday School.

(if he has perfect attendance!)

However, there is greater potential in the teaching of the Word of God to change that child's life!

Therefore, many Christian educators today feel that we should be . . .

"REDEEMING THE TIME, BECAUSE THE DAYS ARE EVIL."

EPH. 5:16

. . . and use every minute that the learner is in the classroom for teaching the BIBLE.

If the learner is involved in the lesson from the moment he enters the room until the moment he leaves, this is called . . .

In the past, the Sunday–school session was structured like this . . .

THE BOX REPRESENTS THE TOTAL TIME THAT A CHILD IS IN SUNDAY SCHOOL.

Generally, there were 15-30 min. for opening exercises in a department time, followed by 50-60 min. of class time.

Opening exercises consisted of...

...SINGING

...RECOGNITION OF BIRTHDAYS

...TAKING OFFERING

Usually this time was unrelated to the lesson that followed.

If total session teaching was utilized, the time might be arranged in the same way, EXCEPT . . .

. . . instead of an opening exercise, one teacher would introduce the lesson to the learners. Then the learners would continue the study of the lesson in their small classes.

This arrangement is only one time arrangement for total session teaching.

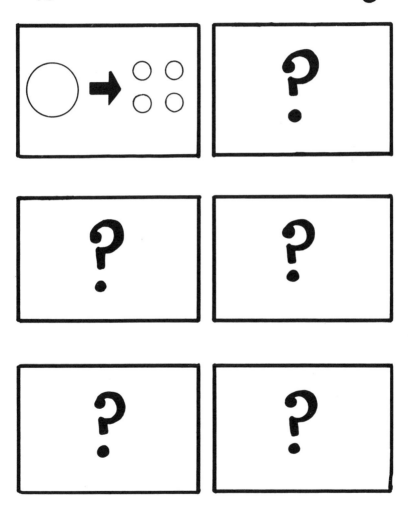

There are six possible arrangements of time in total session teaching.

(O = Department time. 88 = Class time.)

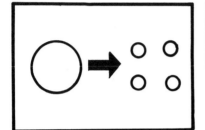

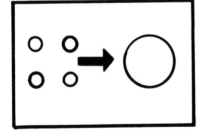

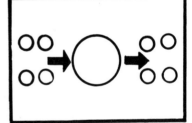

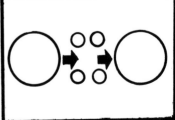

In Sunday school each age division utilizes the arrangement of time that is best suited to its learners.

The Children's (GRADES 1-6) Division basically uses two arrangements, since younger age levels need a more stabilized class structure.

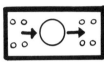

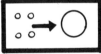

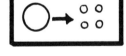

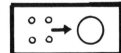

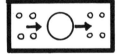

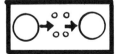

The Adult & Youth (grades 7-12) Divisions use all six arrangements.

What kinds of
activities take
place in each
of these six time
arrangements?

In the Children's Division, every Sunday in a unit would look like this...

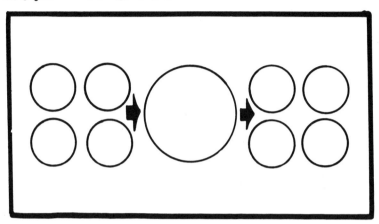

...except the final Sunday of a unit would look like this.

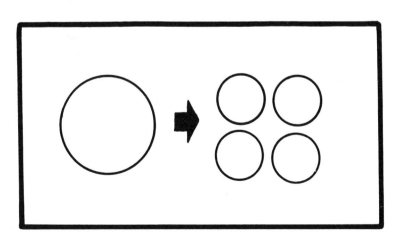

Generally, this is what would happen in those time arrangements:

PRE-SESSION ACTIVITIES...

...THEN STORY TELLING AND SONGS RELATED TO THE LESSON...

...THEN BIBLE LEARNING ACTIVITIES SELECTED BY LEARNER.

...and the final Sunday of a unit:

COMPLETION OF BIBLE LEARNING ACTIVITIES...

PRESENTATIONS OF BIBLE LEARNING ACTIVITIES.

If you teach grades 7-12, any of the six time arrangements could be used...

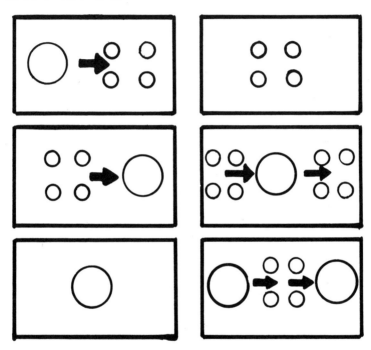

Next, you will see examples of what could happen in each of the six time arrangements for grades 7-12.

Arrangement of time

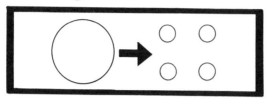

Possible activities:

Film followed by...

...a discussion of the film in small groups.

OR

Ten-minute lecture introducing lesson followed by ...

...research and completion of a worksheet.

Arrangement of time

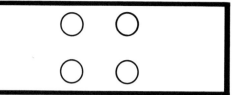

Possible activities:

✳ INDUCTIVE BIBLE STUDY

✳ CREATIVE ART PROJECTS LIKE A MURAL

✳ PRACTICING AND PREPARING FOR A PLAY

Arrangement of time

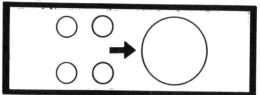

Possible activities:

Learners study
Scripture and plan a
skit that shows the
application of that
Scripture to the
learner's life then...

...skit presentations
and summary.

OR

Each class study the Bible
story and make a poster of
it then...

...the drawings could be
presented to the large
group.

Arrangement of time

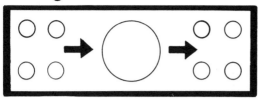

Possible activities:

Pre-session activities . . .

. . . then story-telling and songs related to the lesson . . .

. . . then Bible learning activities selected by learner.

OR

Preparing a group drawing based on a Bible story . . .

. . . then presenting the group drawing

. . . then discussing the application of the Bible story.

Arrangement of time

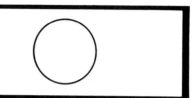

Possible activities:

Panel discussion
followed by questioning
from audience

Special speakers

Field trip

Film shown, followed
by large group discussion

Arrangement of time

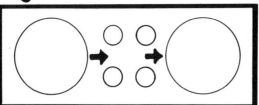

Possible activities:

Filmstrip introducing lesson...

...discussion of Scriptures relating to lesson...

...reports from each group of their conclusions.

OR

Role play introducing lesson...

...completion of work sheet while studying Bible story...

...concluding hymn or song related to lesson.

If you teach in the
Adult Division, you also
have a choice of any of
the six time arrangements.

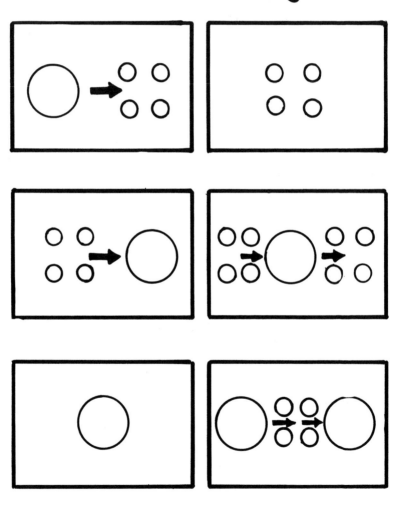

How does a teaching
team determine which
time arrangement
to use?

The arrangement of time is determined by the learning activities that are selected.

Therefore, the time arrangement is an OUTGROWTH of the learning activities that are chosen.

* filmstrip, discussion, reports from discussion groups = [◯ → ° ° → ◯]

* field trip = [◯]

* Introductory lecture, then research = [◯ → ° °]

In summary, total session teaching

redeems the time

by using every minute that the learner is in the classroom to teach Bible content & application.

TEAM PLANNING

When teachers teach together, they need to meet regularly to Plan the lessons together.

Generally the best meeting place is the church *building*...

. . . and at a time when you are already at the church.

* TIME FOR TEAM PLANNING

☐ Before or after weekly prayer meeting

☐ During prayer meeting

☐ Before Sunday evening service

☐ ?

Some teams meet weekly and some teams meet every two weeks.

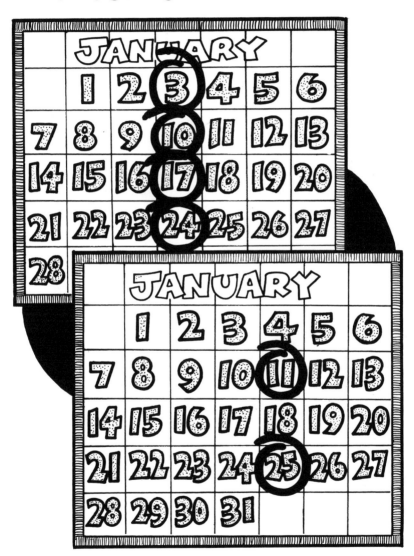

Before teachers arrive at the team planning session they need to . . .

...Study the Scripture for the lesson(s)

...and look over all the teacher's resources.

Posters

TEACHER'S MANUAL

VISUAL AIDS

CASSETTE TAPES

Here are some of the things teachers do in team meeting...

...<u>evaluate</u> the lesson(s) since the last meeting, sharing successes as well as problems.

During the team meeting teachers identify the main idea of the Bible lesson(s) and how it relates to their own lives.

Teachers discuss the AIMS presented in their curriculum. Then they select or adjust the aims for their learners.

AS A RESULT OF THIS LESSON, I WOULD LIKE MY LEARNERS TO

KNOW: _____

FEEL: _____

DO: _____

Ways to teach the lesson are discussed, using ideas from the curriculum and adding any creative ideas agreed on by the team.

IDEAS FROM CURRICULUM

* Flannelgraph Story
* Game for review
*

BRAINSTORMING OTHER WAYS TO TEACH

* Drama of BIBLE Story
* Newspaper of BIBLE Story
* Puzzle for Memory work

Finally, teachers select learning activities. They discuss timing and assign responsibilities as decisions are made.

LESSON PLAN

LESSON *[illegible handwriting]*

LESSON *[illegible handwriting]*

[illegible handwriting]

[illegible handwriting]

CLASSROOM ACTIVITIES

TIME	MINUTES	GROUPING	ACTIVITIES
9:15 9:30	15	○ ○ ○ ○	GREET CHILDREN AND SHARE IN FRIENDSHIP.
9:30 10:05	35	○ ○ ○ ○	BIBLE STUDY IN INDIVIDUAL CLASS —STORY "PETER'S DENIAL OF CHRIST" —DISCUSS APPLICATION OF STORY TO LEARNER'S LIFE — MEMORY VERSE
10:05 10:20	15	○	DEPARTMENT LEADER A) Leads Songs related to application of Bible Lesson B) Reinforces Bible Story through a game
10:20 10:45	25	○ ○ ○ ○	UNIT BIBLE LEARNING ACTIVITY Newspaper___ mr. Jones Drama ____ mrs. Smith Frieze ____ mr. Anderson Cartoon Strip_ mr. Hollis.

To review, team meetings are utilized to:

- ☑ Evaluate previous lesson(s).
- ☑ Identify the main idea of the Bible lesson(s) and how it relates to their own lives.
- ☑ Select aim for their learners.
- ☑ Brainstorm and select the best methods of teaching the lesson(s).
- ☑ Discuss timing of lesson and assign responsibilities.
- ☑ Write an outline of the lesson plan as it is decided.

As decisions are made during the planning meeting, teachers write them on planning sheets.

LESSON PLAN

1. LESSON TITLE _____ AGE LEVEL _____
2. UNIT TITLE _____
3. UNIT AIM _____
   _____

4. BIBLE PASSAGE(S)_____
5. THE MAIN IDEA OF THE BIBLE PASSAGE _____
   _____

6. AIMS. AS A RESULT OF THIS LESSON. I WOULD LIKE MY STUDENTS TO:

    KNOW: _____

    FEEL: _____

    DO: _____

7. CLASSROOM ACTIVITIES:

TIME	MINUTES	GROUPING	ACTIVITY

This planning sheet is usable for all age levels and all class structures.

An agenda should be followed in order to plan the lesson in a minimum amount of time. If you meet weekly, your agenda may look like this...

AGENDA

WEEKLY TEAM MEETING (1½ hrs)

1. Prayer... * For learners
              * For team members
2. Evaluate previous lesson.
3. Discuss Scripture & its meaning
4. Agree on aims (may want to adapt aims in curriculum)
5. Brainstorm ways to teach.
6. Choose classroom activities for lesson from brainstorming list (#5) and teacher's guide.
7. Discuss timing and assign responsibilities.

If you meet every two weeks, double the planning time and plan two lessons instead of one.

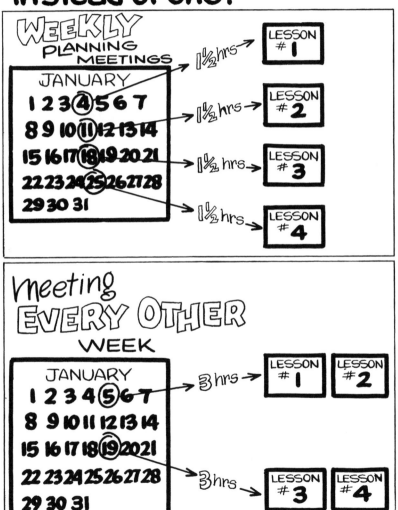

REMEMBER

The team meeting is practical in helping the teachers plan the next lesson. Almost all of the time is spent in actual lesson planning, not administrative details.

REMEMBER

During the meeting the Department Leader is in charge. He guides the discussion during the team meeting.

(HE DOES NOT **Monopolize** IT!)

REMEMBER
Much time needs to be planned for each teacher to relate to his own small group or class.

REMEMBER

As the team plans, it incorporates each teacher's special abilities.

Team planning is exciting because...

...you have help in putting your lesson together,

...you can bounce your ideas off of others, and they can help you evaluate your ideas,

. . . your learners learn more because the team effort has created a better lesson plan,

FINAL EXAM

A+

. . . and team planning is more creative than planning and teaching alone.

You'll discover that you do have strengths as a teacher and you'll grow by adding the strengths of others to your teaching.

ADVANTAGES AND DISADVANTAGES OF A TEAM APPROACH

A team approach provides advantages for...

...The Learners

...the Teacher

...the Congregation

WHAT ARE THE ADVANTAGES OF A TEAM APPROACH FOR

THE LEARNERS ?

Learners are usually grouped according to age. They can also be grouped according to interests, abilities, and level of knowledge.

Learners tend to learn more because instruction is better.

The learners receive more individualized instruction and attention.

The learners can relate to more than one teacher.

WHAT ARE THE ADVANTAGES OF A TEAM APPROACH FOR

THE TEACHER?

Each teacher on a team contributes his own ideas; this gives freshness and variety in planning.

In a teaching team each teacher can use his own special abilities.

Teachers can share insights about students in order to know them and instruct them better.

There are fewer discipline problems.

There is a personal growth within each teacher. Each teacher grows...

...in TEAChING SKills

...as a Christian ✝

IXΘΥΣ

...in Interpersonal Relationships

WHAT ARE THE ADVANTAGES OF A TEAM APPROACH FOR THE

CONGREGATION?

A team approach provides an apprenticeship program for training new teachers.

Current teachers develop new skills and concepts as they teach on a team, so a type of "in-service" training is provided.

Studying the Bible and then discussing it together each week deepens Christian growth and fellowship.

Team teaching has a
way of building in
substitutes, so that...

...Many times it is
unnecessary to get a
substitute and continuity
in the lesson is not
destroyed.

A team approach assures more adequate preparation in the teaching ministry of the church.

Teachers are easier to recruit since the responsibility for teaching is shared.

There are
also Problems in
a
Team approach

Team teaching is time Consuming!

Planning takes more time
But
leads to better instruction

Some people are too insecure to work on a team.

So! Assure each team member that he will not have to lead large group activities until he is ready.

Sometimes team members find it difficult to work together.

So! Remember, there are a few teachers who will work better alone.

The teacher-learner relationship may be endangered.

So! Assign every learner to a particular teacher and Provide considerable involvement between a teacher and his own learners.

The advantages to a team approach far out weigh the disadvantages

therefore, your Sunday School would greatly benefit from a team approach on any age level!

How Can I begin a teaching team?

Begin a teaching team by informing other teachers.

Information can be given by...

...asking teachers to read books about team teaching,

... showing a film strip in a teachers' meeting,

...inviting a resource person to explain team teaching.

A tremendous amount of information can be given through asking teachers to observe a teaching team in a nearby church.

After your teachers have been given information about a teaching team, form a team of interested teachers.

Select your best and most enthusiastic teachers as Department Leaders

Then choose team members who COMPLEMENT each other in temperament, skills, and abilities.

Recruit one teacher for every 8 learners, based on the average attendance.

(NOT ENROLLMENT)

8 learners = 1 teacher

16 learners = 2 teachers

24 learners = 3 teachers

32 learners = 4 teachers

40 learners = 5 teachers

There should be a maximum of...

...**30** learners per team in grades **1-6**,

...**35** learners per team in grades **7-12**

After a team has been formed, ask each team member to read a selected book on team teaching.

Then conduct an initial team meeting...

... to discuss the team concept and roles of team members,

DEPARTMENT LEADER

DEPT. SECRETARY

TEACHERS

...to distribute curriculum materials,

POSTERS

RECORDS

TEACHER'S MANUAL

BOOKLET

...to select a permanent meeting time

MARCH

		1	2	3	4
5	6	7	8	9	10	11
12	13	14	15	16	17	18
19	20	21	22	23	24	25
26	27	28	29	30	31	

...to have the team commit themselves to support each other and devote the time needed to minister to their learners

Teachers plan for the next meeting...

...by studying the Scripture for the lesson,

...by looking over the curriculum materials for the lesson.

POSTERS

TEACHERS MANUAL

BOOKLETS

SONGS OR RECORDS

FILMS

CASSETTE

After the initial meeting, follow the agenda and principles for team planning as suggested in Chapter 5.

During the first few meetings the team will rely greatly on the guidance of the Department Leader as he puts into effect the principles of team teaching.

As teaching teams begin to work together they will grow...

...in teaching skills

...as a Christian

...in interpersonal relationships

...and many *Advantages* of teaching teams will be realized in Your church.

You will see advantages for your *learners...*

Learners tend to learn more

Flexibility of grouping according to interests, abilities, or level of knowledge.

More individualized instruction and attention

Relate to more than one teacher

You will see advantages for your *teachers...*

Freshness and variety in planning

Special abilities of each teacher can be used

Insights about learners can be combined

Fewer discipline problems

Personal growth in each teacher

You will see advantages for your *Congregation*...

Provides an apprenticeship program for new teachers

"In-Service" training for current teachers

Deepens Christian fellowship

Fewer substitutes needed with little loss of continuity in lessons

More adequate preparation in the teaching ministry of the church

Easier to recruit teachers

God will bless the teaching team as they unite their efforts to . . .

. . .lead learners to Christ

and help learners mature as Christians.